TRYTHIS!
Collecting

Stephanie Turnbull

A+
Smart Apple Media

Published by Smart Apple Media, an imprint of Black Rabbit Books
P.O. Box 3263, Mankato, Minnesota, 56002
www.blackrabbitbooks.com

Printed in the United States of America, at Corporate Graphics
in North Mankato, Minnesota.

Designed and illustrated by Guy Callaby
Edited by Mary-Jane Wilkins

Cataloging-in-Publication Data is available from the Library of Congress

ISBN 978-1-62588-371-1

Photo acknowledgements
t = top, b = bottom, l = left, r = right, c = center
page 1 Stefano Tinti; 3 Maria Dryfhout; 4t Svetlana Lukienko,
l Dan Kosmayer, b Victor H; 5t FedeCandoniPhoto, l Diana Taliun,
r Tarzhanova; 6 Alexander Gospodinov; 8t maigi, b scyther5;
9 LiliGraphie/all Shutterstock; 10; 11; 12; 13t all Mim Waller,
b Africa Studio; 14 Dja65/both Shutterstock; 15 Mim Waller;
16l photka/Shutterstock, r frame Yong Hian Lim, girl Jozef Sedmak/
both Thinkstock; 17 Mim Waller; 18t Guzel Studio, b wolfman57/
Shutterstock; 19 Mim Waller; 20 Fine Shine; 21r cosma/both
Shutterstock; 22t sattva78, b stephanie Connell;
23 somen/all Shutterstock
Cover top right aquariagirl1970, background rainbow33, main image
maxik/all Shutterstock

DAD0062b
012016
9 8 7 6 5 4 3 2

Contents

Why try collecting?

**Collecting is a fantastic hobby.
Here are a few reasons to try it!**

1 It's fun to do.

Building up a collection keeps you
busy and brightens up your bedroom.
If friends collect the same things,
you can trade and help each other.

*Your collection could fit inside
one jar or fill your whole bedroom!*

2 It doesn't cost a fortune.

Some people collect rare, expensive items, but you don't have to—how about marbles, pencil sharpeners, magnets, or buttons? Search your house for stuff, ask your family for help, or look in thrift stores.

*Look out for new items to add to your collection, whether unusual **antiques** or shells from the beach.*

3 It looks great.

Displays of items such as ornaments, stones, or bottles can look very stylish, especially if you arrange them well and keep them tidy.

4 It's all about YOU!

Collecting is about keeping things that make you happy, whether they're souvenirs, memories of fun times, or objects you treasure. Think about what you love and start collecting!

Now test out the brilliant projects in this book and see for yourself how exciting collecting can be. Look out for the helpful tips and extra ideas.

Cool containers

Store your collection safely and neatly so nothing gets lost or broken. Here are some good ways to do this.

1 *Find big jars, vases, cans, cups, or bowls to fill with small things such as gems, toy cars, erasers, or beads.*

Glass containers are good because you can see inside. Sort items by size, color, or style.

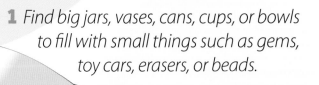

Label boxes and tins so you know what's in them.

2 Buy stackable storage bins or tubs that don't take up too much space. These are great for bigger toys.

3 Make containers for pens and pencils by wedging toilet paper tubes into a small cardboard box.

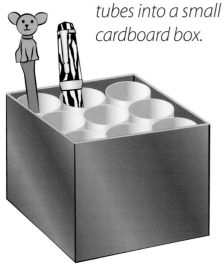

Now try this

Decorate containers to make them look special. Try painting clay plant pots with **acrylic paints** or covering cans with pictures cut from magazines.

Wall displays

If you don't have much shelf space, collect things you can display on the wall, such as photos, postcards, and pictures.

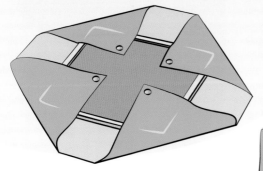

1 *To make a great wall display, find a cork board and a rectangle of fabric big enough to cover it.*

2 *Stretch the fabric over the board and pin the four corners on the back with thumb tacks.*

3 *Fold in the sides of the fabric and tack them in place, too.*

4 *Add a short length of ribbon to hang up your board.*

5 Now place a long piece of ribbon diagonally across the front of the board. Tack it in place on the back.

6 Add more ribbon on either side, then repeat in the other direction to make a criss-cross pattern. Push in thumb tacks at each cross.

7 Hang up your board and tuck photos, tickets, and other **mementoes** under the ribbon.

Now try this

Frame photos, certificates, and paper collections and fill a wall with them. Mix different frames to make your display more interesting.

Ask an adult for help if you need to fix hooks in the wall.

Amazing albums

If you run out of wall space for photos and pictures, keep them in a neat album instead.

1 *Find a sheet of thin cardstock and mark a line of equal size rectangles, each big enough to hold a photo.*

Label photos with where and when they were taken.

2 Cut across the long edge.

3 Neatly fold along each line to make an accordion.

4 Make more strips. Tape the ends together to make one long accordion.

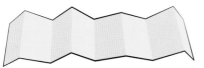

The number of strips you add depends on how many photos you want to put in.

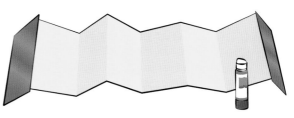

5 Cut two pieces of thick card bigger than your folded pieces. Glue to the end panels to make a cover.

6 Glue a strip of ribbon across the back so you can tie the album shut. Now glue in photos and other things.

Now try this

Buy a **scrapbook** and fill it with photos, tickets, **souvenirs**, stickers, and decorations. **Mount** photos on colorful cardstock to make them stand out more, or cut them into different shapes with **pinking shears**.

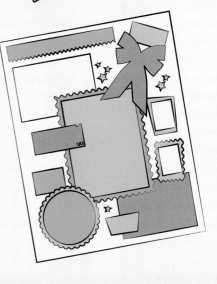

Handy hangers

Some collections, such as key rings, medals, or jewelry, are perfect for hanging up. Here are a few clever methods.

1 *Make a fabric-covered board like the one on pages 8-9, then stick colorful pins in the front. Dangle a key ring from each.*

2 *Mug trees are great for hanging collections. Wind ribbon around them or decorate with paint and stickers.*

Hang several things on each hook or pin to save space.

3 Make **mobiles** by dangling objects from coat hangers. You could also bend the coat hanger into a boomerang shape…

… then hang it on a door knob to hold magazines or comics. Wind **pipe cleaners** or wool around it as decoration.

Now try this

Glue clothes pins to the edges of a cork board and clip key rings and other things in them. Decorate the pins to make them more stylish.

Fabric fun

Try simple sewing to create your own soft felt holders for precious collections.

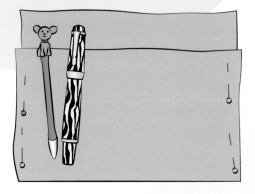

1 *To make a pen holder, cut a large rectangle of felt. Fold it up to make a pocket and pin the edges together.*

Lay your pens on top to make sure they fit.

2 *Thread a needle with brightly-colored thread and knot the end. Stitch carefully along the edges, going up and down through both layers. Take out pins as you go. Finish each line of stitching with a knot inside the pocket.*

3 *Divide the pocket into roughly equal sections. Mark them with pins.*

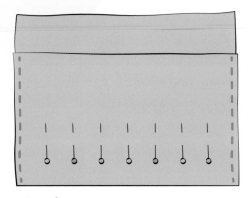

Try to keep stitches neat and straight. Be careful with sharp needles and pins.

4 *Stitch along each line, through both layers of felt.*

5 *Slot in your pens. Roll up the fabric and tie a piece of ribbon, wool, or cord around it.*

Now try this

Follow steps 1 and 2 to make a few felt pockets, then pin them on a cork board. Use them to store stationery collections.

Add extra stitches for decoration.

Colorful collages

A great way of displaying many small items is to make them into a fantastic collage.

1 *Arrange flat collections such as leaves, pressed flowers, stamps, or stickers in a pattern on cardstock, then carefully stick them in place when you're happy with the design.*

Create a picture to frame and hang on the wall, or decorate a photo frame.

The bigger the objects, the stronger the glue needed. White **craft glue** usually works well.

2 *Use larger items such as beads, shells, and shiny stones to cover jewelry boxes or plant pots.*

3 *Sew buttons on felt. Start by marking out a shape or letter with pins.*

Sew on a few big buttons as an outline, then remove the pins. Fill in the gaps with lots of smaller buttons.

Now try this

Turn a collection of buttons, ribbon, beads, and other materials into a scene! Cut pieces of fabric and pin them on felt, then sew in place.

Clever cushions

Start a collection of badges, brooches, or sew-on patches, then display them on stylish home-made cushions.

1 *Find an old, colorful T-shirt. Using the same color thread, stitch up the bottom of the T-shirt. Go through both layers and sew along the **seam** to hide your stitches.*

2 *Stitch up the arm holes in the same way.*

End each line of sewing with a neat knot on the back of the T-shirt.

3 *Fill the T-shirt with pillow stuffing, cotton wool, or other soft material such as old towels or socks.*

4 *Sew up the neck along the seam. Pin on badges and brooches, or sew on fabric patches.*

Add lots of badges to make
your cushion look cheerful.

Now try this
Make extra badges by layering felt
shapes, putting a button on top and
sewing it all together.
Use a small piece
of felt to fix a safety
pin on the back.

PROJECT 8

Great garlands

**Bead and button collections are easy
to thread on wool or cord and hang up.
Others link together to make chains.**

1 *Collect colorful rubber bands, then join them.
Start by squeezing one into a loop, like this.*

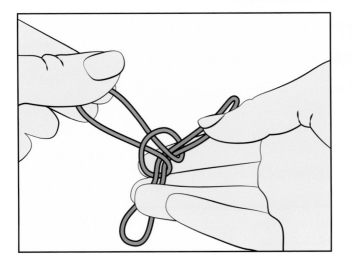

2 *Wrap a second
looped band up
and over it, then
pull one end
through the other
to make a knot.
This secures the
end of your chain.*

3 *Feed another looped band through the ends of the first loop.*

4 *Feed another through the ends of that one. Keep going until your chain is really long. Finish by tying a last band as in step 2.*

Try using several bands to form each link.

Collect bright paper clips and make them into chains to hang above your desk. Keep adding more so the chain grows.

Hang garlands high up so they don't get in the way.

Glossary

acrylic paints
Fast-drying paints that can be mixed with water or used straight from the tube. Be careful, as they won't wash off clothes when dry!

antique
An old, beautiful, well-made object.

collage
A collection of materials, artistically arranged and glued down.

craft glue
Strong, water-based glue.

felt
Soft fabric made from matted, pressed wool. Felt comes in different colors and doesn't fray (unravel) when cut into shapes.

memento
A souvenir or reminder of a person, place, or event.

mobile
A decoration made from hanging objects that turn freely in the air.

mount
To fix something in place on a background (such as a piece of card) to display it.

pinking shears
Scissors that have blades with zigzag edges, like a saw, so they cut a wavy pattern.

pipe cleaners

pipe cleaner
A piece of wire covered with fuzzy material. You can buy packs of colorful pipe cleaners in craft shop

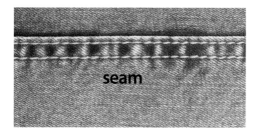

seam

scrapbook
A book of thick, blank pages for sticking in photos and paper souvenirs. Some scrapbooks are very expensive, but you can buy a cheap one and decorate it yourself.

seam
The join where two pieces of fabric are sewn together.

Web sites

http://collectibles.about.com/od/morecollectible categories/u/CollectiblesA-Z.htm
Look at an A–Z list of pretty much everything you could ever think of collecting!

http://lifestyle.howstuffworks.com/crafts/paper-crafts/ paper-desk-organizers.htm
Try making easy desk organizers for all kinds of stationery collections.

www.kidsloverocks.com/html/guide_to_collecting.html
Read interesting tips for starting a collection of rocks and minerals.

Index